YOUR KNOWLEDGE HAS VALUE

- We will publish your bachelor's and master's thesis, essays and papers

- Your own eBook and book - sold worldwide in all relevant shops

- Earn money with each sale

Upload your text at www.GRIN.com and publish for free

Bibliographic information published by the German National Library:

The German National Library lists this publication in the National Bibliography; detailed bibliographic data are available on the Internet at http://dnb.dnb.de .

Imprint:

Copyright © 2008 GRIN Verlag, Open Publishing GmbH
Print and binding: Books on Demand GmbH, Norderstedt Germany
ISBN: 9783640473762

This book at GRIN:

http://www.grin.com/en/e-book/140267/aktionsart-and-its-interplay-with-voice

Tobias Rösch

Aktionsart and its Interplay with Voice

GRIN Publishing

GRIN - Your knowledge has value

Since its foundation in 1998, GRIN has specialized in publishing academic texts by students, college teachers and other academics as e-book and printed book. The website www.grin.com is an ideal platform for presenting term papers, final papers, scientific essays, dissertations and specialist books.

Visit us on the internet:

http://www.grin.com/

http://www.facebook.com/grincom

http://www.twitter.com/grin_com

Albert-Ludwigs-Universität Freiburg, Englisches Seminar

HS: The Syntax and Semantics of the English Verb Phrase

WS 2007/08

Aktionsart and its Interplay with Voice

submitted by

Tobias Rösch

English (SE): 8

German (SE): 8

The present paper is concerned with the interfaces between the verbal categories of *aktionsart* and voice. Despite the fact that *aktionsarten* have been known since antiquity[1], there still seems to be a certain amount of both terminological and conceptual confusion with respect to *aktionsarten*.[2] A general definition most linguists can agree on involves the notion that *aktionsart* (which in most publications is referred to as lexical aspect) basically represents an immanent property of the verb assigning temporal information to a given lexical item.[3] Lexical aspect differs from grammatical aspect in that it is restricted to verb semantics[4]; neither does it include subdivisions based on conjugated forms of a verb, nor does it take into account the syntactico-semantic processes found on the sentential level. Thus, the term *aktionsart* includes procedural characteristics such as "phasal structure", "time extension" or "manner of development" (cf. Bache 1982: 70). Verbal classification is primarily based on specific temporal parameters like telicity, boundedness and the extension on the timeline (i.e. durative aspect as distinct from momentaneous aspect). Vendler differentiates between four semantic types of verbs maintaining that verbs generally fall into categories expressing

a) activity, b) accomplishments, c) achievements, or d) states[5]. While verbs of the a and b categories permit continuous tense, those of the categories c and d do not.[6] Although activities and accomplishments can both be described as durative actions stretching over an extended period of time, only the latter terms exhibit a terminal point at which, as soon as it is reached, the action comes to an end. Activity terms, by contrast, do not support a terminus or present the action as culminating at a specifically identifiable point in time; instead, here the action goes on homogeneously (that is, each and every stage of the ongoing process is on par with the process as a whole, e.g. in activity verbs like running or swimming) for an indeterminable length of time.[7] Terminative processes

---

[1] Cp. Ziegeler, Debra (2006): *Interfaces with English aspect: diachronic and empirical studies*, p. 7
[2] The term *"aktionsart"* was coined in 1885; in German linguistics, however, it usually has a much wider meaning; cp. Kortmann, Bernd (1991): "The Triad Tense-Aspect-Aktionsart: Problems and Possible Solutions", p. 13
[3] More precisely, *aktionsart* is concerned with situation-internal time, cp. ibid., p. 14
[4] Cp. Comrie, Bernard: (2002): "Some thoughts on the relation between aspect and aktionsart." In: Barentsen, A.; Poupynin, Y. (eds.) *Functional Grammar: Aspect and Aspectuality. Tense and Temporality*, p. 43
[5] Cp. Vendler, Zeno (1967): *Linguistics in Philosophy*. Ithaca, NY: Cornell, p. 102f.
[6] Cp. ibid., p. 104
[7] Cp. ibid., p. 101

2 2

are usually referred to as being telic, while non-terminative processes are described as atelic. Another distinction that is often wrongly equated with the telic/ atelic relation is that of boundedness and unboundedness. States of affairs (SoA) can be presented as bounded when they are complete and no longer in progress.[8] A telic state of affairs can be presented as unbounded when the verb phrase expresses durativity:

1) a. I made a chair. [+telic, +bounded]   b. I was making a chair. [+telic, -bounded]

The second similarity pair (the members of which have less in common than those included in the activity/accomplishment pair) is that of achievement and state. Neither achievement nor state verbs appear in continuous forms (there is no such thing as "I am knowing" or "I am loving"[9]); however, achievement verbs refer to a single instant in time, whereas state verbs refer to a longer time segment.[10] Therefore, a sentence like "John reached the summit." cannot be (sensibly) conceived as implying that John started reaching the mountain peak the very moment he began to climb the mountain.[11] Instead, the predication focusses on the instant that terminates John's climbing (which, of course, is telic, as you can hardly climb a mountain without reaching the top at some point, unless we assume a premature abortion of the action). States are generally defined as static (see, for example, Comrie 1976[12]): they "continue as before unless changed, whereas events and processes are dynamic". Comrie's definition of stativity, however, does not include a very small class of predicates that express point states, for example "be 5 o'clock" or "be on time". They semantically refer to a single point in time which has no extension beyond the given time specification (e.g. "5 o'clock" or an appointed time, as in "be on time").[13]

The examples we have used so far (1a, b) are sentences in the active voice, with an agent in the subject position. In active sentences, sentential aspect is not exclusively construed by means of the semantic properties of the main verb, but also by the subsequent complement it takes. For example, in

2a) Mary walked a kilometre.

---

[8] Cp. Guerrero Medina, Pilar (2001): "Reconsidering aspectuality: interrelations between grammatical and lexical aspect.", p. 7
[9] As in the well-known McDonald's slogan "I'm lovin' it", state verbs can exceptionally appear in the continuous form for emphasis!
[10] Cp. Vendler, Zeno (1967): *Linguistics in Philosophy*. Ithaca, NY: Cornell, p. 115
[11] Cp. ibid., p. 104
[12] Cp. Comrie, Bernard (1976): *Aspect*. Cambridge et al.: Cambridge University Press, p. 13
[13] Cp. Croft, William: "A two-dimensional analysis of lexical aspect.", p. 6

the terminative reading is not established by the verb, as "walk" in itself has a durative meaning that does not contain a terminal point (i.e. walking as a repetitive process of lifting and dropping your feet continuously). Only its complement, "a kilometre", which in Verkuyl's terminology is a "specified quantity of A" [SQA][14] indicates a termination of the action.

The SQA adds a terminative meaning to the whole sentence, presenting the action (perfec-tively) as forming a complete whole and leaving no doubt that the process of walking has come to an end after the specified length of one kilometre. The temporal and spatial extension given by the conjunction of verb and complement indicates that the moving entity, here "Mary," (the "Theme") is in a process of movement which covers a certain distance between a starting point (the "Source") and an end point (the "Goal"), which we could call the "Path".[15] By adding the specifying complement "a kilometre", the durative activity of walking is transformed into a terminative activity with a climax.

In order to analyze a sentence for terminativity, it has been suggested to add either a container adverbial ("in" + a time specification) or a durative adverbial ("for" + a time specification):

       3a) #Judith ate a sandwich for an hour.   3b) Judith ate a sandwich in an hour.

The sentence in 3a is interpretable in two ways: Through forced stretching of the event the expression could imply that it took Judith sixty minutes to eat a sandwich. On the other hand, the action of eating could be considered to be repetitive (and probably discontinuous), meaning that Judith only occasionally took a bite of a sandwich during the length of an hour.

Active sentences like 3) "Judith ate a sandwich." normally consist of at least a subject, a verb and a direct object (for example, there are also sentences with two objects, e.g..: "John gave [Mary$_{ind. obj.}$ [the book$_{dir. obj.}$.")[16] In order to transform the active sentence into a passive sentence, most Indo-European languages have developed a periphrastic construction involving a stative auxiliary (English "be", f. ex.), a dynamic auxiliary ("get" or "become",

---

[14] Cp. Verkuyl, Henk (1993): *A Theory of Aspectuality*, p. 17
[15] Cp. Verkuyl, Henk (1993): *A Theory of Aspectuality*, p. 15
[16] For the sake of simplicity we will restrict ourselves to the analysis of the most basic structure containing only one direct object.

as in Norwegian), or both (as in Polish). At the clause level, three major changes take place:

1. the active subject is demoted to a passive agent; 2. the active object is promoted to subject in the passive construction[17]; 3. (in dynamic passive sentences) the initiator is expressed through a by-phrase. Additionally, the auxiliary "be" is followed by the past participle of the main verb (which is sometimes referred to as "passive participle")[18].

By juxtaposing both sentence types it becomes obvious that the semantic value of the verb phrase is altered; instead of only one verb, as in the active sentence, we find two verbs (that is, an auxiliary and a main verb) in the passive sentence. What consequences does passive morphology have in terms of meaning construal?

Functionally, the verb "be" is either used in the role of an auxiliary or in that of a proper main verb. In some cases, however, it is impossible to determine, whether a sentence has a stative or a dynamic meaning. Cp.: 4a) The bottle is broken.

This sentence allows for two readings: One is stative, the other is dynamic (or, more precisely: resultative).[19] Thus, 4a) can be understood as presenting the subject's condition; it does not touch on the question whether the state described was caused by the action of an agent.

As the condition of brokenness generally presupposes a preceding condition of intactness,

it would certainly be wrong to posit that the bottle might have never formed a complete and undamaged whole, and it is therefore justifiable to assume that before the bottle could be described as broken, an action or event must have occurred which has transformed the bottle's state of intactness into one of brokenness. It is this intervention of an external agent (and not so much the resultant state) the second interpretation focuses on; at the end of the sentence, one could easily add a by-phrase indicating the initiator of the destructive action:

4b) The bottle is broken by Tom / a bullet, etc.

---

[17] This process of shifting positions is generally called passivization: some linguists believe that the passive subject develops out of the verb complement. Radford, A., Atkinson, M., Britain, D., Clahsen, H., Spencer, A.
(1999): *Linguistics. An introduction.* Cambridge: Cambridge University Press, p. 334
[18] Cp. ibid., p. 333
[19] Cp. Dimitrova-Vulchanova, Mila (1999): *Verb Semantics, Diathesis and Aspect*, p. 111

Consequently, the readings of the sentence oscillate between what could be translated into an active sentence as either "the bottle is in a broken state" (where "broken" is an adjective, not a past participle) or "an agent breaks the bottle." In 4a) we can therefore detect either a stative or a transitive resultative construction. As there are no formal distinctions mirroring the semantic differences, such ambiguities can merely be resolved by the context.

Informal English adds yet another facet to the bandwidth of different meanings conveyed by auxiliaries in passive sentences: oftentimes "be" can be replaced by "get" to indicate passive voice. However, these two lexical items are not as congruent with one another as it may seem: unlike "be", "get" is used especially when the referent of the subject is accountable for the state of events.[20] The sentence "He was killed in gunfire." does not imply any kind of valuation on the part of the speaker, but "He got killed in gunfire.", particularly when used in conjunction with a reflexive pronoun ("himself"), carries the idea that the subject is in some way responsible for his fate.

The phenomenon of get-passive, which is less common in written formal English[21], is usually found in connection with verbs that have a dynamic meaning. As in Vendler's distinctive features underlying the grouping of verbs into four semantic categories, the most prominent opposition in passive sentences is that of dynamic versus stative. Not only does this differentiation affect the way passive sentences can be interpreted, but also that sometimes there are even restrictions to a set of verbs that impact on the structural level.

The so-called "middle verbs", a number of stative transitive verbs, for example, are predominantly (and sometimes exclusively) used in active constructions[22]: Although it is possible to say "They have a nice garden," the passive equivalent #"The garden is had by them," can hardly be deemed grammatical. While middle verbs represent lexical items confined to the active voice, most of the other verbs in the English language can be used in active and passive sentences alike. Another restriction concerns intransitive verbs, i.e. verbs that are monovalent and have the subject as their only argument: in their exclusion from passive sentences intransitive verbs are similar to middle verbs: A sentence like "Henry died." cannot possibly be transformed into a passive sentence

---

[20] Cp. Quirk, Randolph; Greenbaum, Sidney (1990): A Student's Grammar of the English Language, p. 45
[21] Cp. ibid.
[22] Cp. Quirk, Randolph; Greenbaum, Sidney (1990) A Student's Grammar of the English Language, p. 45

(#"Henry was died."), as intransitives lack the direct object required for the process of passivization.[23] Moreover, the verb „die" is hard to classify with Vendler's criteria; it could present both an accomplishment and an achievement. Dying can be conceptualized as an accomplishment because it is bounded in time, i.e., referring to a process that necessarily ends with a person's death. At the same time, however, the verb may also refer to the specific point in time in which the vital functions fail and the person is considered dead. Although formally the verb clearly bends towards the category of accomplishment verbs (as it does appear in the continuous form), both inter-pretations (terminative and momentaneous) are conceivable.

Aktionsart has a number of contact points with voice. As becomes clear in Verkuyl's discussion of Vendler's verbal categories, analyzing verbs in isolation and without taking into account the semantic properties of their complements can hardly be deemed a practicable approach. Sometimes the temporal structure of an action is only sufficiently developed through the combination of a verb (phrase) and its subsequent complement. The present work has illustrated that diathesis and *aktionsart* are intertwined insofar as both are dependent on verb semantics. The English language, however, has a grammatical voice rather limited in scope when compared to languages like Russian, Slavonic or Irish. In these languages, the passive voice is not only characterized by a syntactic rearrangement of subject and object roles, but here diathesis has also the function of a perfect marker.[24]

In closing, it is quite obvious that the concept of *aktionsart* is legitimate, and not only in the Slavonic languages that morphologically distinguish between durative and non-durative verbs. However, and on this point I agree with Henk Verkuyl, it is inevitable to draw a clear dividing line between aspect and *aktionsart*, in order to avoid a differentiation that is too inexplicit and indistinct in its outline.[25]

---

[23] Cp. Radford, A., Atkinson, M., Britain, D., Clahsen, H., Spencer, A. (1999): *Linguistics. An introduction*, p. 334
[24] Cp. Comrie, Bernard (1976): *Aspect*. Cambridge et al.: Cambridge University Press, p. 84
[25] Cp. Verkuyl, Henk (1993): *A Theory of Aspectuality*, p. 11

Works Cited

1) **Comrie**, Bernard: (2002): "Some thoughts on the relation between aspect and aktionsart."
> In: Barentsen, A.; Poupynin, Y. (eds.) *Functional Grammar: Aspect and*
> *Aspectuality. Tense and Temporality. Essays in Honour of Alexander*
Bondarko
> (LINCOM Studies in Theoretical Linguistics, 23). Munich: LINCOM
Europa.
> p. 43-50.

2) **Comrie**, Bernard (1976): *Aspect.* Cambridge et al.: Cambridge University Press, 151 pp.

3) **Croft**, William: "A two-dimensional analysis of lexical aspect."
> http://www.unm.edu/~wcroft/Papers/Verbs1.pdf

4) **Dimitrova-Vulchanova**, Mila (1999): *Verb Semantics, Diathesis and Aspect.*
> Munich/Newcastle: LINCOM Europa, 200 pp.

5) **Guerrero Medina**, Pilar (2001): "Reconsidering aspectuality: interrelations between
> grammatical and lexical aspect." Presented at 9th International Conference
on
> Functional Grammar, Madrid 20-23 september 2000.
> home.hum.uva.nl/fg/working_papers/wpfg75.html.

6) **Kortmann**, Bernd (1991): "The Triad Tense-Aspect-Aktionsart: Problems and
Possible
> Solutions". In: Vetters, C.E.; Vandeweghe, W. (eds.): *Belgian Journal of*
> *Linguistics* 6. (Proceedings of the International Symposium 'Tense - Aspect
–
> Aktionsart' Louvain-la-Neuve 1990), p. 9-30.

7) **Quirk**, Randolph; **Greenbaum**, Sidney (1990) *A Student's Grammar of the English*
> *Language.* Harlow: Longman, 490 pp.

8) **Radford**, A., **Atkinson**, M., **Britain**, D., **Clahsen**, H., Spencer, A. (1999):
Linguistics.
> *An introduction.* Cambridge: Cambridge University Press, 438 pp.

9) **Vendler**, Zeno (1967): *Linguistics in Philosophy.* Ithaca, NY: Cornell, 218 pp.

10) **Verkuyl**, Henk (1993): *A Theory of Aspectuality: the Interaction Between Temporal and*

      Atemporal Structure. Cambridge: Cambridge University Press, 411 pp.

11) **Verkuyl**, Henk (1972): *On the Compositional Nature of the Aspects.* Dordrecht: Kluwer,

      204 pp.

12) **Ziegeler**, Debra (2006): *Interfaces with English aspect: diachronic and empirical studies.*

      Amsterdam: Benjamins, 325 pp.

YOUR KNOWLEDGE HAS VALUE

- We will publish your bachelor's and master's thesis, essays and papers

- Your own eBook and book - sold worldwide in all relevant shops

- Earn money with each sale

Upload your text at www.GRIN.com and publish for free